RHYHEIM: A PORN POEM

I0111179

Vikram Kolmannskog (b. 1980) is a writer, psychotherapist, and professor of gestalt psychotherapy. He has a mixed heritage with a Norwegian father and a mother born in Kenya to Gujarati parents. He lives outside Oslo together with his husband Daniel.

www.Vikram.no

Also by Vikram Kolmannskog

Rhyheim:
a porn poem

Vikram Kolmannskog

Broken Sleep Books

ISBN: 978-1-915760-59-3

The author has asserted their right to be identified as the author of this Work
in accordance with the Copyright, Designs and Patents Act 1988

Cover designed by Aaron Kent

Edited and Typeset by Aaron Kent

Broken Sleep Books Ltd   Broken Sleep Books Ltd
Rhydwen   Fair View
Talgarreg   St Georges Road
Ceredigion   Cornwall
SA44 4HB   PL26 7YH

Contents

I'm 18 or older

THUNDERBOLT

Big black
As big
As this
Stanza
But first
When I patiently
Watch from
The start:
Small-talking in
A white bedroom
A young white guy
Putting on white
Fishnet tights asks
So what is your
Posting schedule like?
I'll post this tomorrow
Or tonight
Oh really?
I'm fast
Cool
What about you?
Rhy asks
While trying
To put on a necklace
Lucas continues
I like your necklace
Thank you
Like a baby Rhy   laughs
                 A sharp short inhalation like
                 Norwegians sometimes say yeah
                 And then exhaling heh
                        It's the cheapest thing but I like it
Lucas helps Rhy

On the bed
Rhy sits
Smoking a joint
Legs spread
Lucas slowly takes
Some of the cock
In his mouth
Smoke spreads
Earth, fire, pine

Facing him
I too let Rhy in
He fits perfectly
Big black cock penetrating
Light through tiny pupils
The size of three grains of sand
His sweet laughter causing
Ripples in a snail shell-like cochlea
He is lightning in my night sky
Incredible intimacy
Him and I

And because I want to
Another guy appears
Licking my nipples
Smelling my armpits
Sandalwood sweat
All four of us now
Relaxing in Rhy's bright big bed
I watch us all
A flatscreen on the white wall

The fishnet tights
Torn open
A pink tongue
Like a strange sea-animal
Long and strong
Strokes up against
A greyish pink
Pearl-like asshole

Rhy doesn't manhandle
His way in
He merely
Places himself
So the cock
Incredibly erect is
Just outside Lucas' hole
A continent
Not to conquer
Rather:

A light touch
Then some more
Longing but
Waiting
To be invited in

Lucas takes it
In his own hand
Just a little inside
Relaxes, opens
Let's go

Continents are still
In movement today
The Himalayas growing
Earth in patient play

Rhy's body is smooth
Warm dark brown in the cool white room
Like the soft rumbling
Ohhh yeahhhhhh
That comes from Lucas
Deep down

Rhy watches
Lucas' eyes half-open
Biting his pink lips
Opening his mouth
Facing each other
Reflecting, rotating, revolving
Like the moon and the sun
Right here

A candle shines
On the floor
Scented perhaps
What do they smell now?
Earth, fire, ocean, pine?

Dark honeycomb-like clouds form
Over, inside and all around
Drops on his awesome face shining
Brilliant black cock crashing
Veins flashing
Rhy lifts him up
Puts him down
Stretches his long arm and places
A pillow under his head

I remember
As a child
I loved watching
The lightning outside
Counting thousand and one
Thousand and two
Thousand and three
Thousand and four
Thousand and five
Thunder cracking
With my dad
Safe for now inside

In the midst of the raging storm, Rhy
Smiles
The most awesome flash seen anywhere
Indestructible wisdom and care
Holding and filling soul-flesh there
Here, everywhere

THREESOME

                                        Rhy is behind
                    Isaac sucking
Cade's cock
They switch
Rhy in front
                                        Cade behind

                    Licking looks
                    Up at Rhy
                    Eyes smile
Rhy sits up
          Stretches his left arm
                    Towards Cade
               Cade moves up
Next to Rhy
Lips
Tongues
Butterfly wrestling
Big cocks resting

Isaac takes Rhy's
Rhy bends down
Sucks Cade for a while
Moves up
Abs
Chest
Nipples
Mouth

A small
Palm tree on
right flank

Isaac's

A Hebrew
Tattoo
On his left

A massive
Cross on
Cade's   right shoulder

His mom
Nancy
On his left

Rhy licks
Isaac kisses
Rhy lubes
Good boy
Cade's cock
There you go

Rhy stretches
Kisses Isaac's ear
Further to Cade
A hand on his neck
Kissing, fucking on
My kitchen table
A dull Norwegian November day

Outside across the hedge
My neighbour looks
Like Cade Kent
A special police force guy
Perhaps I should hide
Let's play
I find a place
Behind Isaac's palm

Rhy embraces Cade
From behind
Left hand around his left hip
Sliding onto his abs
Stroking
Up to his chest
Kissing his neck while

Cade fucks

Isaac from behind

His right hand on his cock
Close to Cade's right hip
Cade's ass as he ever-so
Slowly fucks
Against Rhys' left thigh

In bed
My boyfriend Dan's
White bubble-butt ass
Pushes against my brown cock
I rush
But then
Remembering my guru Rhy
Slow eyes
Kind kissing
Lips
Tongue
Taking time
Dan and I
Here and now
So hot

         And sometimes Rhy

                Joins us

                He fucks him

                While kissing me

                We switch

         But then I sense someone actually watching

In the corner
Anita sits quietly
She's sneaked into the room
And it's a little weird
But then, old and wise, she stares into space, apparently
And I half-pretend she's not exactly here

                Looking at him

                Come

Immediately afterwards I
Look over at her with a smile
Come come

EVERYONE

You fuck young white men
And older white men
But you also invite others
Sharok
Angel
Elijah
To hang out around a pool
In your friend's L.A. garden
And Dane
East-Asian
Barely nineteen I like to think
Floating naked on a white thing
The sight of him is like
The smell of kumquat
In the shade on a hot day
And you come out of the house
Striding tall and lean
Confident as an elephant
Cock swaying and swinging
Up to Dane
Dane who sits on a white towel now
You light up a joint
I'm gonna get a tan today
Laughter bonding and
A slight bow to you

Everyone stands in a close circle kissing
While Dane kneels in the centre
Sucks one cock, then another
Banana trees, bright sunshine
Different sizes and shapes and shades
Dane smiles
You bend down
Lick his hole
Bougainvillea screams
Deep purple into the sky

We go to the spa
Outside Oslo
Surrounded by
Large, dark trunks
Evergreen pine trees in white snow
Undress, shower
And wrap ourselves in white bathrobes
Which we take off again as we enter the Finnish sauna
Where an older white man, grey really, sits in a peshtemal
While a younger couple, a black man and a white woman, sit naked
Close together on white towels as he massages
Her shoulders, her head between his legs, and I want to
But I don't touch Dan
In this hot, dry silence
And when I go to the shower I hope
They'll join me
But what I see in the shower is
A white, wrinkled body
Sagging skin, tiny dick
The older white man from before
And our eyes meet and
As a young man
I
I!
I!!
Would have hated him for this
But middle-aged myself now I know
Where we are all going so
I let him look
Suck my cock
In his mind
While I lick Dane's pink hole
And watch the male-female couple fuck
And he leaves me semi-hard

Dan enters the shower and I think
Fuck it, this spa is owned by one of us
Hagen, which means garden
And the pine trees and snow don't judge
And I move close to him
And he fondles
My big queer cock just
For a moment
And I take his queer hand
Walk out past
The male-female couple and the rest
To the toilet
Where everyone fucks
And afterwards
As we get dressed
Dan says
You had the second biggest cock there
I meant biggest
And we laugh
Back home I measure
Seven and a half

You fuck the way
A meditation master does
Hours and hours of practice
Or non-practice
Just being and enjoying perhaps
Not just for yourself
But for all beings
Letting go, knowing
Sunshine sings through limbs
Soil saturates soul
Nothing to worry about
Nowhere to go
There is only fucking
No fucker separate from fucking

Fucking as effortlessly
As a butterfly flaps its wings
Participating in all sorts of amazing things

The ease of Earth
And other planets
Revolving

The thrusting
Hips are
A sutra
Celebrating
Enjoying
Just like
Trees growing
Birds singing
Sun shining
Earth and
All planets
Revolving
The whole universe
And beyond
Doesn't everything make love?
A brilliant black fucking song

I'm not putting you on a pedestal
What stands still
Will fall

I could worship you
Your cock
Like millions do
And sometimes I do
But I'm also learning
To look deeper
To praise more of you
Praise the sunshine in your lunch, flesh, skin, smile
Praise the air you breathe in and out
All the plants you breathe together with
Praise marijuana
Praise the ground that holds you
Praise the river rushing through, water, blood, spit, semen, piss
Praise Nancy
Praise all parents
Praise Hebrew
Praise all languages
Praise silence
Praise darkness
Praise light
Praise everything we consist of
Praise everything we are
Praise everything we do

More than a statue
A drifting, shifting cloud
A slowly growing tree

Plunging into Dane
Amidst green fern
The sun grips him tightly
A breeze loosens the grip for a bit
A lotus opens
Four pink petals
Tender and strong

Dane is divine
Immaculate body of
Shit and sunshine
Fuck yeah
Rushing up his spine
Out of his eyebrows spring
Seduction, pain, pleasure, joy, everything

Elijah's fingers over his face
One slightly enters his mouth
Rapidly my hand from cock to
Spacebar stop
Zoom in on the deliciously tanned hand and nails
Dark brown, mint green and white
A screenshot
I paint my nails too
Before I know he's your
Real-life partner
Now I notice how you look
At each other, how he keeps glancing up at you
Rings on right hand ring fingers
Your right hand on your cock now
As you jerk yourself off I notice how
The Norwegian-Pakistani couple glance down at
My light blue and white nails
When I first meet them on the street and say hi, I'm Vikram
And welcome them
To this mostly middle-class, straight and white neighbourhood
I don't mind
I, no more alone and afraid than a white cloud
Right now part of the vast blue sky
I don't hide
I know your face
Divine pride
We smile

You all hold each other
Naked by the pool
Arms around necks
Dane lying down
And you, great Rhy, come
Like a leaf falling through
The air
Silently

Sharok, Angel and Elijah bend in
On themselves
And Dane waits
Hundreds of thousands of viewers wait
A neighbour laughs
You can hear the sun burn
You can hear the planet turn
And the poet
Why pretend, I mean I
Wanting to find a fitting image
To describe this painful scene
Keep thinking about it
Looking at the poem
Looking at the porn scene
Remembering similar episodes from my own life
Again and again
But it won't come
I tense
To get the image
To get the poem done but
The lily knows
It depends on sunshine, rain, soil, everything
The lily doesn't spring
Into a white flower
Just because a vain gardener
Wants to show off to
Visitors who have come from far away
Just because he waters the lily extra much today
Only humans can be this silly
Putting so much faith in an erected I
Can we hear the chirping laughter?
Juvenile rats in rough-and-tumble play
Can we hear the rat in a cage not far away?
A human tickles him on his tummy and nape

He laughs and
Seeks out the hand
A playmate
Again and again this game
But suddenly he is lifted up
Removed by the same hand, wearing a glove
Placed on an elevated platform
Blinding light
Tickled
But he doesn't laugh
It's not the same
Afraid, sad and alone
The scientist-human believes in evolution
But doesn't even know
The great rat's true name
Doesn't even know
They are friends
While
Elijah
Sharok
Angel
And I
Try
Do we remember that time?
The boy child wanting to show off to his friends
Sit
And it's a big dog
But it's still a puppy
And the puppy wants to play
And the boy child repeats
Sit
And the puppy has done it before
Sit
And his friends look at him

Sit!
But the puppy looks away
Sit!!
And one of the friends just wants to say
And you do, Rhy, right now you say

                                        It's okay

Angel comes and
Shows his biceps
Still a young man
Victory and strength

Yet each person, relationship and situation is
Not necessarily a battleground

Sharok and Elijah continue to jerk off but then
They look at each other and laugh
Sharok hands Dane
A towel

They go in the pool
You join them

A paradise and playground today

Sharok lifts Dane and kisses his stomach and chest
A small black dog appears at the edge of the pool
Reminding me of Anita
Elijah holds his hand in front of her eyes, laughing
Sharok climbs onto
The small guy carries the big man around
Thanks daddy, laughing
The dog kisses Sharok on the mouth and jumps in

                                        Splash

A wave of consciousness
The sound
The hearing
The hearer
One

While writing this poem
While watching your porn
Anita, so kind and wise
She died in December

                              She's always by my side

A white wolf-like dog
Watches and listens
Just near the pool

I realize now you must say the name
So many times a day
Shouting sternly to keep Shiva by your side
Shaking your head as Shiva zooms around the house
Shiva is stubborn but melts you with laughter and smile
Whispering Shiva affectionately at night
Going to bed in the bright white room
Shiva sleeping in a bed next to yours
Shiva as subtle sound in your mind

I'll share a secret
Ash white, auspiciously wild
In the kitchen
In the bed
In the spa
Fucking
Big
Small
Young
Old
Just as I come
To remind myself
To direct the energy
This is what
I finally
Say

Thousand and
Now I know that you and I
Meet intimately
In this sound
Always
Here
      Dog
                God
Scratched behind the ear

Sometimes after
The lightning smile

Sometimes after
Coming cloudy white on a pink hole, then pushing it inside

Sometimes after
Hehe

Sometimes after
Fuck yeah

Sometimes after
The fresh smell of pine

Sometimes after
The musky smell in pubic hair

Sometimes after
The taste of tangy-salty sperm

Sometimes after
The touch of the cool breeze

Open, clear

AFTERWORDS

I am learning
The easy way

A powerful thunder-clap
Gradually fading away

To fully listen to any enchanting sound
Cessation of chattering chitta mind

To meditate on the beauty of the visible
And after it fades away, letting

Awareness remain
Open and clear

Invigorated by the sense of
Immediate being

Be unattached
Or be like Buddha
Attached to
Everything

Such is Shiva
Bhairava

-

These lines are based on verses 14-19 of
Svabodhodaya-mañjarī (*The Blossoming of
Innate Awareness*) as translated by
Christopher Hareesh Wallis, available at
https://hareesh.org/blog/2018/3/9/the-blossoming-of-your-awareness

I've had enough sex in my lifetime for probably 10 lifetimes. I'm honest enough to admit now that sex for me is enjoyed vicariously. Whether through my partner or audience, my pleasure comes more from empathy now than self-gratification. I really don't have much interest—and, to be honest, much time or energy—in casual sex anymore.

From the outside looking in, that can seem kinda sad, but for me it's the opposite. To have so much power taken away from my hormones is kind of freeing. But hey, if I connect with someone on "that" level, fuck a camera. Let's get naked.

— Rhyheim Shabaz, *Str8UpGayPorn*, 20 April 2019,
https://str8upgayporn.com/rhyheim-shabazz-gay-porn-star-timtales/

Acknowledgements

Thank you to Aaron Kent and Broken Sleep Books for believing in this book!

Thank you to everyone who creates poetry and literature! I have especially appreciated, and felt supported by, the erotica traditions in gay literature and Indian classical literature.

Thank you to all the gay porn stars and Rhyheim Shabazz in particular!

Thank you to my husband Daniel Gjerde Kolmannskog! I am immensely grateful for all the sexiness, wisdom, and care.

LAY OUT YOUR UNREST

www.ingramcontent.com/pod-product-compliance
Lightning Source LLC
LaVergne TN
LVHW041236080426
835508LV00011B/1240